To
Father Tom
Happy 130ᵃ Jesuits in Trinidad
Anniversary
Gene and Monika Bond

Christmas
with Dietrich Bonhoeffer

Edited by Manfred Weber

Augsburg Books

MINNEAPOLIS

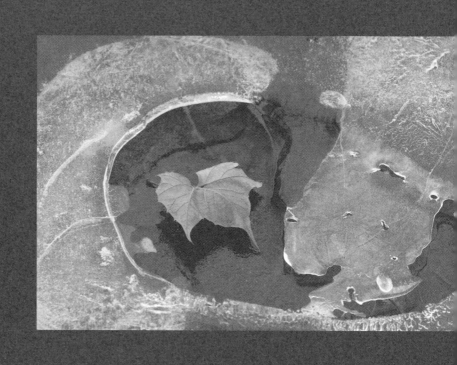

This reversal of all things

If we want to be part of these events,
Advent and Christmas,
we cannot just sit there like a theatre audience
and enjoy all the lovely pictures.
Instead, we ourselves will be caught up
in this action,
this reversal of all things;
we must become actors on this stage.
For this is a play in which each spectator has
a part to play,
and we cannot hold back.
What will our role be?
Worshipful shepherds bending the knee,
or kings bringing gifts?
What is being enacted
when Mary becomes the mother of God,
when God enters the world
in a lowly manger?

We cannot come to this manger
in the same way that we would approach
the cradle of any other child.
Something will happen to each of us
who decides to come to Christ's manger.
Each of us will have been judged or redeemed
before we go away.
Each of us will either break down,
or come to know that God's mercy is turned
toward us....
What does it mean
to say such things about the Christ child?...
It is God, the Lord and Creator of all things,
who becomes so small here,
comes to us in a little corner of the world,
unremarkable and hidden away,
who wants to meet us and be among us
as a helpless, defenseless child.

God's mercy

Celebrating Advent

means being able to wait

Celebrating Advent means being able to wait.

Waiting, however, is an art

that our impatient age has forgotten….

We must wait

for the greatest, most profound,

most gentle things in the world;

nothing happens in a rush,

but only according to the divine laws

of germination and growth and becoming.

Promise

At Christmas, God's great promise
is to be fulfilled.

In the birth of Jesus Christ,
God took on
the form of all humanity,
not just that of a single human being.

The birth of Jesus Christ

Our living as real human beings,
And loving the real people next to us
is, again, grounded only in God's becoming human,
in the unfathomable love of God
for us human beings.

God becomes human

God becomes human
out of love
for humanity.
God does not seek the most perfect
human being
with whom to be united
but takes on human nature
as it is.

out of love

Christ has taken on

this human form

Christ has taken on this human form.
He became a human being like us.
In his humanity
and lowliness
we recognize our own form.

Jesus Christ

Jesus Christ,
the God who became human –
this means
that God has bodily taken on
human nature in its entirety,
that from now on
divine being can be found
nowhere else
but in its human form,
that in Jesus Christ human beings are set free
to be truly human before God....
In becoming human,
God is revealed as the one
who seeks to be there
not for God's own sake
but "for us."

When God in Jesus Christ
claims space in the world –
even space in a stable
because "there was no other place in thc inn"–
God embraces the whole reality of the world
in this narrow space
and reveals its ultimate foundation.

the God who became human

The miracle of all miracles is
that God loves the lowly....
God is not ashamed
of human lowliness,
but goes right into the middle of it,
chooses someone as an instrument
and performs miracles right there,
where they are least expected.

God travels

God travels wonderful paths
with human beings;
God does not arrange matters
to suit our opinions and views,
does not follow the path
that humans would like to prescribe for God.
God's path is free and original
beyond all our ability
to understand or to prove.

wonderful paths

A new ordering

of all things

on this earth

When God
chooses Mary as the instrument,
when God wants to enter this world
in the manger in Bethlehem,
this is not an idyllic family occasion,
but rather the beginning
of a complete reversal,
a new ordering of all things on this earth.

The manger and the cross

There, where our understanding is outraged,
where our nature rebels,
where our piety fearfully
keeps its distance—
there, precisely there, is where God loves to be.

For those who are great
and powerful in this world,
there are two places
where their courage fails them,
which terrify them to the very depths of their souls,
and which they dearly avoid.
These are the manger and the cross
of Jesus Christ.

Jesus Christ

Joy abides with God,
and it comes down from God
and embraces spirit, soul, and body;
and where this joy has seized a person,
there it spreads,
there it carries one away,
there it bursts closed doors.
A sort of joy exists
that knows nothing at all
of the heart's pain, anguish, and dread;
it does not last,
it can only numb a person for the moment.
The joy of God has gone through
the poverty of the manger
and the agony of the cross;
that is why it is invincible,
irrefutable.

The shepherds

The shepherds, like the wise ones from the East,
stand at the manger
not as converted sinners,
but simply because
they have been drawn to the manger
just as they are.

the wise ones
from the East

Miracle

of miracles

No priest,
no theologian
stood at the cradle of Bethlehem.
And yet all Christian theology
finds its beginning
in the miracle of miracles,
that God became human.

A son

This text speaks
of the birth of a child,
not the revolutionary deed
of a strong man,
or the breath-taking discovery
of a sage,
or the pious deed
of a saint.
It truly boggles the mind:
The birth of a child
is to bring about the great transformation of all things,
is to bring salvation and
redemption to all of humanity.

As if to shame
the most powerful human
efforts and achievements,
a child is placed in the center
of world history.
A child born of humans,
a son given by God.
This is the mystery of the redemption of the world;
all that is past and all that is to come
is encompassed here.

given by God

A child has our lives in his hand....
Most likely many
in our old, clever, experienced,
self-assured world
shake their heads
and even laugh with contempt,
when they hear,
"For a child has been born for us,
a son given to us."

The entire weight

"Authority rests upon his shoulders."
Authority over all the world is to rest
on the weak shoulders
of this newborn child!
One thing we know:
in any case these shoulders
will have to bear the entire weight of the
world....
But the authority will consist in this,
that the one bearing this load does not
collapse
but rather brings it to its goal.

of the world

God became

human

"Wonderful-Counselor"
is the name of this child....
In the form of a human child
God gave us God's Son,
God became human,
the Word became flesh.
That is the wonder
of the love of God for us,
and it is the unfathomable, wise counsel
that this love wins and saves us.

God became a child

"Mighty God"
is the name of this child.
The child in the manger
is none other than God.
Nothing greater can be said:
God became a child.

"Everlasting-Father"–
how can this be the name of the child?
Only in that
the everlasting fatherly love of God is revealed
in this child
and that the child desires nothing else
but to bring the love of the Father to earth….
Born within time,
he brings eternity with him to earth;
as the Son of God
he brings to us all
the love of the Father in heaven.

Born within time

"Prince of Peace"–
where God comes in love to human beings,
becomes united with them,
there peace is secured
between God and human beings
and between one human being and another.

Presence

"Wonderful Counselor,
Mighty God,
Everlasting-Father,
Prince of Peace"–
this is how we speak
at the manger in Bethlehem,
this is how our words
pile up on one another
at the sight of the divine child, ...
Yet these words
are finally in fact nothing other
than a wordless silence of adoration
before the inexpressible,
the presence of God
in the form of a human child.

of God

In a Bethlehem

stable

For the good of all humankind

Jesus Christ

became human

in a Bethlehem stable.

Rejoice,

oh Christendom.

All who at the manger
finally lay down
all power and honor,
all prestige,
all vanity,
all arrogance and self-will;
all who take their place
among the lowly
and let God alone be high;
all who see the glory of God
in the lowliness
of the child in the manger:
these are the ones who will truly
celebrate Christmas.

Source Credits

All excerpts are taken from *Dietrich Bonhoeffer Werke* by Dietrich Bonhoeffer. 17 vols. Edited by Eberhard Bethge et al. Munich and Gütersloh: Chr. Kaiser/Gütersloher Verlagshaus, 1986–99. English translation: *Dietrich Bonhoeffer Works*. 17 vols. Wayne Whitson Floyd Jr., General Editor. Minneapolis: Fortress Press, 1996–.
Excerpt from page 17 comes from DBW 4: *Nachfolge*. Edited by Martin Kuske and Ilse Tödt. Munich: Chr. Kaiser, 1989; 2d ed., Gütersloh: Chr. Kaiser/Gütersloher Verlagshaus, 1994. English translation: *Discipleship*. Edited by Geffrey B. Kelly and John D. Godsey. Translated by Barbara Green and Reinhard Krauss. Minneapolis: Fortress Press, 2001, page 285.
Excerpts from pages 14, 15, 18, 19 come from DBW 6: *Ethik*. Edited by Ilse Tödt, Heinz Eduard Tödt, Ernst Feil, and Clifford Green. Munich: Chr. Kaiser, 1992; Gütersloh: Chr. Kaiser/Gütersloher Verlagshaus, 2d ed. 1998. English translation: *Ethics*. Edited by Clifford J. Green. Translated by Reinhard Krauss, Charles C. West, and Douglas W. Stott. Minneapolis: Fortress Press, 2004, pages 87, 84–85, 400, 63.
Excerpt from page 27 comes from DBW 8: *Widerstand und Ergebung*. Edited by Christian Gremmels, Eberhard Bethge, and Renate Bethge, with Ilse Tödt. Gütersloh: Chr. Kaiser/ Gütersloher Verlagshaus, 1998. English translation: *Letters and Papers from Prison*. Edited by Wayne Whitson Floyd Jr. Translated by H. Martin Rumscheidt, Lisa Dahill and Reinhard Krauss. Minneapolis: Fortress Press, forthcoming, page number not yet available.
Excerpts from pages 11, 12 come from DBW 10: *Barcelona, Berlin, Amerika 1928-1931*. Edited by Reinhard Staats and Hans Christoph von Hase, with Holger Roggelin and Matthias Wünsche. Munich: Chr. Kaiser Verlag, 1991. English translation: *Barcelona, Berlin, New York: 1928-1931*. Edited by Clifford J. Green. Translated by Douglas W. Stott. Minneapolis: Fortress Press, forthcoming, pages 529, 584.
Excerpt from page 41 comes from DBW 12: *Berlin: 1932-1933*. Edited by Carsten Nicolaisen und Ernst-Albert Scharffenorth. Gütersloh: Chr. Kaiser/Gütersloher Verlagshaus, 1997. English translation: *Berlin: 1932-1933*. Edited by Victoria J. Barnett. Translated by Isabel Best, David Higgins, and Peter Krey. Minneapolis: Fortress Press, forthcoming, page 455.
Excerpts from pages 8-9, 20, 21, 23, 24, 25, 42 come from DBW 13: *London 1933-1935*. Edited by Hans Goedeking, Martin Heimbucher, and Hans-Walter Schleicher. Gütersloh: Chr. Kaiser/Gütersloher Verlagshaus, 1994. English translation: *London: 1933-1935*. Edited by Keith Clements. Translated by Isabel Best. Minneapolis: Fortress Press, forthcoming, pages 341, 339-40, 339, 340-41, 339, 342, 343.
Excerpts from pages 13, 29 come from DBW 15: *Illegale Theologenausbildung: Sammelvikariate 1937-1940*. Edited by Dirk Schulz. Gütersloh: Chr. Kaiser/Gütersloher Verlagshaus, 1998. English translation: *Theological Education Underground: 1937-1940*. Edited by Victoria J. Barnett. Translated by Victoria J. Barnett, Claudia and Scott Bergmann-Moore, and Peter Frick. Minneapolis: Fortress Press, forthcoming, pages 540, 538.
Excerpts from pages 26, 30, 31, 32, 35, 36, 37, 38, 39 come from DBW 16: *Konspiration und Haft 1940–1945*. Edited by Jørgen Glenthøj, Ulrich Kabitz, and Wolf Krötke. Gütersloh: Chr. Kaiser/Gütersloher Verlagshaus, 1996. English translation: *Conspiracy and Imprisonment: 1940-1945*. Edited by Mark Brocker. Translated by Lisa Dahill. Minneapolis: Fortress Press, forthcoming, page numbers not yet available.

Photo Credits
Page 28, © Jürgen Schunck, Coburg
Cover and page 34, © Jürgen Vogt, Mössingen
Page 40, © Peter Santor, Karlsruhe
All other photos: Gütersloher Verlagshaus Photoarchive

ISBN 0-8066-5004-4

First English-language edition published by Augsburg Books in 2005.
Edited by Victoria J. Barnett and Wayne Whitson Floyd Jr.

Original German edition © Gütersloher Verlagshaus GmbH, Gütersloh 2004.
Edited by Manfred Weber.

Cover design: Init GmbH, Bielefeld
Reproduction: redhead, Steinhagen
Printing and Binding: Těšínská Tiskárna, Česky Těšín
Printed in Czech Republic

09   08   07   06   05   1   2   3   4   5   6   7   8   9   10